Life's Big Questions

To my family at Branch Community Church—
I am grateful for the privilege of worshipping
and serving alongside each of you

Life's Big Questions

-Colossians-

Doug Flanders, MD

Prescott Publishing
Tyler, Texas

Life's Big Questions: Colossians
Copyright © 2015, Doug Flanders, MD

Cover design, interior design, and typesetting:
Jennifer Flanders

Cover photos:
Microsoft Office Stock Photos (front)
Jennifer Flanders (back)

Publisher:
Prescott Publishing
3726 Woods Blvd.
Tyler, TX 75707
http://prescottpublishing.org

ISBN: 978-1-938945-12-0
LCCN: 2015935359
.

- Contents -

- Introduction -

The Socratic method of teaching has been around since long before that famous Athenian made it so popular. It is the simple process of asking questions to shed light and enlightenment on a given topic of conversation or study.

One might say that God Himself employed the method when He asked Adam, *"Who told you that you were naked? Have you eaten from the tree of which I commanded you not to eat?"* (Genesis 3:11) Then later, when He asked of Cain, *"Where is Abel your brother?"* (Genesis 4:9)

Jesus likewise employed the technique, often after telling a parable. For instance, after the parable of the Good Samaritan, He turned to the lawyer who had asked, *"Who is my neighbor?"* (Luke 10:29) and responded, *"Which of these three do you think proved to be a neighbor to the man who fell into the robbers' hands?"* (Luke 10:36)

Sometimes, Jesus used the method in response to the Pharisees' efforts at trickery. When they asked Him, *"Is it lawful to give a poll-tax to Caesar, or not?"* (Matthew 22:17), He responded with a famous question of His own, *"Whose likeness and inscription is this?"* on the coin. (Matthew 22:20)

Asking questions turns any monologue into a dialogue, don't you think?

It turns a lecture into a debate, engaging all who are involved on a whole new level. It is a favorite method amongst teachers everywhere, across virtually all times and cultures. It is particularly popular in professional schools where learning to think critically is as important, if not more important, than memorizing facts.

Life's Big Questions: Colossians

The goal of the "Life's Big Questions" series is to get the reader to think critically about the big questions in life and to engage those questions fully. The books can be used for personal study, but they can also be used for family discussions or small group activities, as well.

Since they are intended to provide a starting point for continued study and conversation, these books can be used over and over again. The questions they raise will not change, but the answers you bring to those questions will grow and mature over time. May God bless you as you seek to know and be known, by Him, by yourself, and by those around you.

- Scripture -
Colossians 1:1-12

Paul, an apostle of Jesus Christ by the will of God, and Timothy our brother, to the saints and faithful brethren in Christ who are at Colossae: Grace to you and peace from God our Father.

We give thanks to God, the Father of our Lord Jesus Christ, praying always for you, since we heard of your faith in Christ Jesus and the love which you have for all the saints; because of the hope laid up for you in heaven, of which you previously heard in the word of truth, the gospel which has come to you, just as in all the world also it is constantly bearing fruit and increasing, even as it has been doing in you also since the day you heard of it and understood the grace of God in truth; just as you learned it from Epaphras, our beloved fellow bond-servant, who is a faithful servant of Christ on our behalf, and he also informed us of your love in the Spirit.

For this reason also, since the day we heard of it, we have not ceased to pray for you and to ask that you may be filled with the knowledge of His will in all spiritual wisdom and understanding, so that you will walk in a manner worthy of the Lord, to please Him in all respects, bearing fruit in every good work and increasing in the knowledge of God; strengthened with all power, according to His glorious might, for the attaining of all steadfastness and patience; joyously giving thanks to the Father, who has qualified us to share in the inheritance of the saints in Light.

- Chapter 1 -
A Spiritual Time Capsule

Archaeologists have recently discovered an ancient synagogue on the shores of the Sea of Galilee where they believe Jesus taught. Like most things archaeological, there is a bit of educated guesswork going on. The town is named Magdala, from which Mary Magdalene may have derived her name, and its close proximity to water would have supported a fishing economy, so prevalent in the gospel accounts.

It is unlikely that we will ever know with absolute certainty, but it is still interesting to ponder the possibility that Christ stood right there and spoke the words that changed the course of history!

In similar news, a time capsule buried by Samuel Adams and Paul Revere, two of our nation's founding fathers, was recently unearthed. It was placed under the State House in Boston in 1795 and contains coins, engravings, newspaper clippings, and other documents. It was designed *to be found* and was intended to give future generations insight into the history of our country.

A more modern twist on the time capsule concept is the video time capsule. People will typically videotape themselves talking to their future selves, future children, or future generations. Several movies and books have told the tragic story of people dying from cancer or some other disease who record a video to document their final thoughts or instructions to those who will be left behind.

When Paul penned the epistles that constitute such a large portion of the New Testament, one wonders if he knew that they would eventually become a spiritual time capsule for multiple generations of believers. Certainly, he had specific people and situations in mind. And certainly, with all the beatings, jailings, stonings, and shipwrecks, he knew that death was ever imminent. But regardless of his intentions, God knew how important those letters would be and saw to it that they were preserved.

Before we open up the spiritual time capsule of Colossians to see what Paul has placed inside, let's take a moment to consider what we would put in a time capsule for future generations to find.

- What items would you put in time capsule to be opened in 100 years?

- What if it were opened in 10 years, or 50, or 200? Would the time frame matter?

- What thoughts, ideas, or advice would you want to leave behind, if you found you had only a few months to live?

- Would those thoughts, ideas, or advice be specific to individuals, universal in application, or maybe both?

Chapter 1 – A Spiritual Time Capsule

Now let's look at what Paul placed inside the time capsule of the book of Colossians. Upon examination of this book as a whole, we note that his instructions fall into two broad categories: How we view God and how we interact with our fellow man.

The Ten Commandments can be similarly divided, and when Christ was asked to name the greatest commandment, He answered,

> *"Love the Lord your God with all your heart and with all your soul and with all your mind." This is the first and greatest commandment. And the second is like it: "Love your neighbor as yourself." All the Law and the Prophets hang on these two commandments.* (Matthew 22:37-40, NIV)

- Love God. Love People. Why is this a recurrent theme in Scripture?

- Can you love God without loving people? (see John 13:35, 1 John 4:19-21)

- Can you love people without loving God? (see Proverbs 17:17, Matthew 5:44-47)

- What are some ways to show your love for God? (John 14:15)

- What are some ways to show your love for people? (1 Corinthians 13:4-7, James 2:15-16)

Regarding how we view God, Paul discussed the superiority of Christ: *"He is before all things, and in Him all things hold together."* After discussing this briefly, Paul pointed out a few things that tend to distract us from Christ.

Obviously, distraction was not a problem exclusive to the early Christians. We face similar obstacles today: our distractions may be physical distractions or philosophical distractions.

- What are some simple things in our day-to-day life that can distract us from Christ?

- Are these things inherently bad, or only bad because we give them greater importance than they deserve?

- What are some ideas or philosophies that can distract us from Christ?

- Can good ideas wrongly applied or carried to an extreme become bad ideas or even idolatry?

- Can you think of modern examples of well-meaning people going too far and losing sight of Christ?

- What can we do to help minimize the distractions we face?

Chapter 1 – A Spiritual Time Capsule

Regarding human relations, Paul's advice can be summed up as follows: If you are in authority, show compassion; if you are under authority, show deference.

- What are some situations in your life where you are in authority?

- How can you show Christ-like compassion to those under you?

- If we interviewed those under you, what would they say?

- What are some circumstances where you are under authority?

- Do you tend to play the rebel or have a servant's heart?

- If we had instant replay in life, like they do in sports, what would that show? Would the ruling of the judges support your viewpoint?

These are the big themes in the book of Colossians. In the chapters that follow, we will delve into these themes in greater detail as we carefully explore this spiritual time capsule that remains as culturally relevant today as when Paul first penned it!

– Scripture –
Colossians 1:13-23

For He rescued us from the domain of darkness, and transferred us to the kingdom of His beloved Son, in whom we have redemption, the forgiveness of sins.

He is the image of the invisible God, the firstborn of all creation. For by Him all things were created, both in the heavens and on earth, visible and invisible, whether thrones or dominions or rulers or authorities—all things have been created through Him and for Him. He is before all things, and in Him all things hold together. He is also head of the body, the church; and He is the beginning, the firstborn from the dead, so that He Himself will come to have first place in everything. For it was the Father's good pleasure for all the fullness to dwell in Him, and through Him to reconcile all things to Himself, having made peace through the blood of His cross; through Him, I say, whether things on earth or things in heaven.

And although you were formerly alienated and hostile in mind, engaged in evil deeds, yet He has now reconciled you in His fleshly body through death, in order to present you before Him holy and blameless and beyond reproach—if indeed you continue in the faith firmly established and steadfast, and not moved away from the hope of the gospel that you have heard, which was proclaimed in all creation under heaven, and of which I, Paul, was made a minister.

– Chapter 2 –
The Supremacy of Christ

Paul Harvey tells the story of the man who wakes up on Christmas morning to find a flock of birds stranded in his yard. A storm has blown in and grounded the poor creatures.

Realizing that if he doesn't do something, the birds will all freeze to death, the man quickly puts on his jacket, goes outside, and opens the door to his barn. He then proceeds to try and chase the birds into the barn.

Naturally, the birds just scatter and flee from him. After multiple attempts at enticing the birds into the barn, he thinks to himself, "If only I could become a bird for just a little while, then I could earn the birds trust, explain what needs to be done, and show them the way into the barn." Just as these thoughts run through his mind, the church bells begin to ring and he realizes that is exactly what Jesus did for us!

Christ is our Redeemer, God made flesh. He became a man for a little while that He might lead us unto Himself. He is the bridge between God and man.

What Colossians tells us in this passage is that Christ is more than just the link between God and man, He is also our Creator and Sustainer. How appropriate that the One who made us should also be the One to redeem us!

They say you never fully appreciate flowers until you have planted a few yourself. This is probably true of any creative endeavor: painting, music, writing, dance, sculpture, etc. The process of creating something gives us a special understanding and appreciation of that thing.

- What is something creative you have done or made in the past? Are you working on any current creative endeavors?

- Did you have a deeper appreciation for that art form afterwards? Did you become a fan or an enthusiast?

- Did the thing you made have a special place in your heart or home, even if it wasn't as pretty or professional as other things you own?

- Since Christ is our Creator, do you think He appreciates each of us in a special way? Is He a *people enthusiast*, perhaps? (Psalms 139:13-16; Jeremiah 29:11)

- What are some things we can do to cultivate a Christ-like view of our fellow humans? Would investing in their lives change our perspective?

- Does raising children bring unique insights? Can you give examples?

Chapter 2 – The Supremacy of Christ

Beyond creating us, Christ also sustains us. "In Him all things hold together," says verse 17. The very molecules of our bodies are held together by the power of His will! Isn't that an amazing thought?

But then, Christ goes a step further and reconciles us with the Father, as well. His goal is to present us to God *"holy and blameless and beyond reproach."* (verses 20-22). He is our Creator, Sustainer, and Redeemer.

- If Christ is in the business of restoring and reconciling people, shouldn't we, as Christ's representatives, be in the same business as well? (see Matthew 5:23-24, Galatians 6:1-2)

- Are art preservation and art restoration organizations typically made up of enthusiasts or non-enthusiasts? Fans or haters?

- When we look at our own hearts, are we fans of the people around us? (see Philippians 2:3-4) Do we believe the best, hope the best, and desire the best for each one of them? (1 Corinthians 13:7-8)

- Imagine that a piece of artwork—some beautiful masterpiece—has been damaged in some way and an expert is called in to restore it to its original glory. Do you think the required restoration will be a rough, angry process or a gentle, careful process?

- How are we approaching the people restoration projects God has put into our lives? With gentleness and care or with some other attitude?

- Where are you most likely to be involved in a people restoration project? At home? At work? At church? Does the setting affect how you respond?

- When a piece of artwork is damaged, who is the best person to repair it, the original artist or someone else?

- What does this say about our role in the people restoration process? (refer to 1 Corinthians 3:5-7, Philippians 1:3-6) Are we even an artist or just a paintbrush? A little of both? How does this affect our view of ourselves?

- Does this perspective affect how we view others? How we pray for them? How we treat them?

Chapter 2 – The Supremacy of Christ

Interestingly, Christ is not only the Creator, Sustainer, and Redeemer of all the things we see, but also of all the things we cannot see. It is an interesting point that Paul seems to emphasize and undeniably an important one, considering all the things we cannot see.

We are extremely good at seeing medium sized objects, moving at moderate rates of speed, over short periods of time. But once you begin to examine the vastness of the galaxies, the minuteness of atoms, or the length of eternity, our ability to perceive (much less to understand) begins to break down.

- What are some physical things we know about that we cannot actually see? Hear? Understand fully?

- Are there things we don't even know about yet?

- What about the future? 100 years from now? Next year? Tomorrow? (see James 4:13-15)

- What about the past? Did it really happen the way we were told? Ever play the game gossip?

- Even the present is a mystery, is it not? Do the politicians mean what they say? Are my business associates really being honest with me? Is that marriage as happy as it appears?

- What about spiritual things? The mind of God? The heart of our neighbor? Our own hearts? (see Jeremiah 17:9, Isaiah 55:8-9, 1 Samuel 16:7b)

It is mind boggling to realize that the sum of things we don't know is infinitely greater than all the things we do know. Fortunately, we know the One who knows all and understands all. Because He created all and sustains all, there are no mysteries with Him.

And He is in our corner: He is for us (Romans 8:31). Our God is a people enthusiast, and He is gently working to reconcile mankind to Himself.

- Scripture -
Colossians 1:24–2:5

Now I rejoice in my sufferings for your sake, and in my flesh I do my share on behalf of His body, which is the church, in filling up what is lacking in Christ's afflictions.

Of this church I was made a minister according to the stewardship from God bestowed on me for your benefit, so that I might fully carry out the preaching of the word of God, that is, the mystery which has been hidden from the past ages and generations, but has now been manifested to His saints, to whom God willed to make known what is the riches of the glory of this mystery among the Gentiles, which is Christ in you, the hope of glory.

We proclaim Him, admonishing every man and teaching every man with all wisdom, so that we may present every man complete in Christ. For this purpose also I labor, striving according to His power, which mightily works within me.

For I want you to know how great a struggle I have on your behalf and for those who are at Laodicea, and for all those who have not personally seen my face, that their hearts may be encouraged, having been knit together in love, and attaining to all the wealth that comes from the full assurance of understanding, resulting in a true knowledge of God's mystery, that is, Christ Himself, in whom are hidden all the treasures of wisdom and knowledge.

I say this so that no one will delude you with persuasive argument. For even though I am absent in body, nevertheless I am with you in spirit, rejoicing to see your good discipline and the stability of your faith in Christ.

– Chapter 3 –
Preacher as Pediatrician

A "doula" is a birthing aide or attendant who provides physical and emotional assistance both during and shortly after the delivery of a child.

Doulas rarely have formal training and are most effective when they are not functioning as a "medical professional." Despite their informal role, having a doula in attendance at a birth leads to better health for babies on a variety of levels, ranging from decreased time in the neonatal ICU to more successful nursing after the child is born.

"Birthing assistant" seems like such a perfect analogy for the role Christians play in the spiritual birth of other new believers. For instance, a doula is not responsible for the conception, delivery, or raising of the new child. Her role is limited to that of birthing "aide," "attendant," or "assistant." Yet it proves to be an important and beneficial role, nonetheless.

Interestingly, the word "doula" comes from Greek, like much of the New Testament. Furthermore, it is in the feminine form, and the Church is considered to be the bride of Christ.

However, the most fascinating parallel comes from the actual meaning of the word, which is "slave."

- Is "slave" or "servant" a fitting description of our role in God's kingdom? Why or why not?

- If we are servants, then whom are we serving? God? Fellow man? Both?

- A doula provides "physical" assistance during the delivery process. Can physical assistance be important during "spiritual birth," as well? Give examples.

- Doulas typically are without formal training and function best as non-professionals. How and why might God use "non-professionals" or lay people to further His kingdom?

- If God is responsible for all the "big things" in the spiritual birthing process, what exactly is our role as "aide" or "attendant?" Why and for whom is our role important?

- The doula can help with teaching babies to nurse. When we think of the "milk of the Word," how might this analogy carry over to the feeding of new believers?

Chapter 3 – Preacher as Pediatrician

Of course, birth is just the beginning. Once the child is born, a wide variety of people enter the child's life. One of those people is the pediatrician.

Typically, the pediatrician tries to see the child promptly after delivery to assess the overall health of the child. If there are problems, the pediatrician can intervene. Interventions can range from simple things such as nutritional support to full-scale ICU care with ventilators and blood transfusions.

Otherwise, the pediatrician will simply begin monitoring the child, assessing his growth and development, providing advice, giving preventative vaccines, and treating illnesses as they arise.

As we look at Colossians, it is easy to see Paul as a pediatrician, an under-physician to the Great Physician, who is zealous in his care for the "children of the King." He is writing to a group of young believers who are growing in their faith and facing a variety of challenges.

As he writes to them, Paul is *prepared*. Paul is *purposeful*. And Paul is *passionate*. These are three great qualities for both a pediatrician and a preacher.

- Young doctors have two types of preparation: bookwork and hands on. Though not discussed in this passage directly, in what ways did Paul receive some of each?

- Is one more important than the other? Did God use both in Paul's case? How so?

- Does preparation evidence a lack of faith? What role does the Holy Spirit play?

- Reread verse 29. Does this give some insight into the interplay between preparation and the Holy Spirit?

- Young doctors also specialize. Is preaching a "specialty" within Christian service? What might some other "specialties" be? (See Eph. 4:11) Might an evangelist be a full time "doula," so to speak, distinct from a pastor or preacher?

- What advantage might there be to having a single-minded purpose, such as Paul's to preach Christ? Can we all be that single-minded? Should we be?

- Paul had a unique and literal "calling" from the Lord recorded in Acts. Do you think Paul was passionate because he had been called, or was he called because he was passionate?

- What was Paul like before his calling? (See Phil 3:6)

- Does God take into account our personality, desires, and abilities when He calls us to a specific task?

- Who created those things within us in the first place? Might they actually be part of His directive?

Chapter 3 – Preacher as Pediatrician

Paul also talks about struggling and suffering on behalf of the young Christians to whom he was writing.

- What are some ways we know that Paul struggled and suffered on behalf of others?

- Young doctors are often called upon to struggle and suffer for those they serve. Long hours, sleep deprivation, and exposure to disease are just a few examples. What are some ways a pastor might struggle and suffer for his congregation?

- What are some ways you might be called upon to struggle and suffer for others?

- Will you be willing to suffer when the time comes? Will you rejoice as Paul did in verse 24?

God is calling each of us to serve Him. We may only be part-time birthing assistants or we may be full time preachers.

Whatever our role, we would do well to follow Paul's example of being prepared, purposeful, and passionate.

Colossians 2:6-15

Therefore as you have received Christ Jesus the Lord, so walk in Him, having been firmly rooted and now being built up in Him and established in your faith, just as you were instructed, and overflowing with gratitude.

See to it that no one takes you captive through philosophy and empty deception, according to the tradition of men, according to the elementary principles of the world, rather than according to Christ.

For in Him all the fullness of Deity dwells in bodily form, and in Him you have been made complete, and He is the head over all rule and authority; and in Him you were also circumcised with a circumcision made without hands, in the removal of the body of the flesh by the circumcision of Christ; having been buried with Him in baptism, in which you were also raised up with Him through faith in the working of God, who raised Him from the dead.

When you were dead in your transgressions and the uncircumcision of your flesh, He made you alive together with Him, having forgiven us all our transgressions, having canceled out the certificate of debt consisting of decrees against us, which was hostile to us; and He has taken it out of the way, having nailed it to the cross. When He had disarmed the rulers and authorities, He made a public display of them, having triumphed over them through Him.

– Chapter 4 –
Firmly Rooted

The most extraordinary thing about the tea plant is how extremely ordinary it appears. It is a variation of the common camellia and looks like nothing more than a common bush.

One's first reaction upon seeing it is to think, "Really? That's it?"

There are no distinguishing features, no gorgeous flowers, just a jumble of haphazard branches and a bunch of green leaves. What makes the tea plant special is the fact that the entire plant is permeated with caffeine—especially the leaves.

Caffeine acts as a natural insecticide to make the tea plant resistant to virtually everything that is typically harmful to other plants. Insects obviously stay clear, but so do fungi. Even animals dislike the bitter taste. Deer and rabbits, so harmful to other crops, will eat the weeds all around a tea plant, but leave it undisturbed, thus acting as natural gardeners instead!

The net result is that tea plants can be healthy and productive for hundreds of years (some 600 year old plants are still producing) without the use of external pesticides of any sort.

It's what's on the inside that counts.

That isn't to say tea plants don't require care. They do. Left to themselves, they will grow tall and wild, reaching heights of over fifteen feet with leaves that are high and out of reach.

To be useful, they must be pruned regularly—as often as every three weeks—for their entire lives. They require lots of sunshine, but also lots of rain. The roots, however, are the key.

New plants are cultivated using cuttings from old plants. These cuttings are placed in soil that is saturated with water and contains a root stimulator. Once the roots have begun to grow, the water supply is temporarily cut off.

As the soil dries out, the roots begin to spread deeper and wider, searching for moisture. Then, just before the plant begins to wilt, the master gardener will add a little water, but only enough to keep the plant alive.

This cycle is repeated until the roots are strong and robust. Only when the roots are fully formed can the plant be moved from the greenhouse and placed in the ground. Even then, the tea plant will require three or four years of maturation before harvesting of the leaves can begin.

- Paul speaks of being "firmly rooted" in this passage. What does that mean for the Christian?

- What typically happens to plants whose root systems are not firmly established?

- What are some things that might prevent a plant's roots from growing properly?

Chapter 4 – Firmly Rooted

Typically, the idea of firm roots falls into two broad categories: doctrinally firm and experientially firm.

Being doctrinally firm means having a solid understanding of the basic tenets of Christianity. Being experientially firm means that those basic tenets have been tested personally and have held up under the trials and challenges of life.

- Which does Paul seem to be emphasizing in this passage—doctrinal or experiential firmness?

- Which does James emphasize in James 1:2-5?

- Do some denominations focus on one idea more than the other?

- Do we focus on one idea more than the other in our own lives?

- Are both ideas equally important? Why or why not?

- What are the pitfalls of becoming too focused on only one of these aspects of faith?

- How does the development of doctrinal roots affect or differ from the development of experiential roots? Can you think of ways you might deepen and encourage the development of both?

When we look at the experiential side of being firmly rooted in our faith, the idea of trails and tribulations seems to be a recurring theme in scripture.

- Are trials and tribulations an important part of growing in the faith? Are they a necessary part?

- Like the tea plant above, have you ever experienced "dry spells" in your walk with God? Can you share an example?

- Did God, the Master Gardener, use those times to draw you closer to Him? Did you, in fact, become more firmly rooted in your faith as a result?

- Did you "rejoice" during that time? Can you rejoice now, looking back? Can you imagine a time when you will rejoice at the beginning of a tribulation rather than at the end?

- If larger tribulations deepen our roots, might the smaller trials in life be part of the pruning process? Is frequent pruning necessary or beneficial in the life of a Christian? Why or why not?

- Is it harder or easier to see God at work in these less dramatic trials as compared to the larger tribulations? Should we rejoice, nonetheless?

Chapter 4 – Firmly Rooted

When we look at the doctrinal side of being firmly rooted in our faith, grace is the recurring theme of Scripture:

"For by grace you have been saved through faith; and that not of yourselves, it is the gift of God; not as a result of works, so that no one may boast." (Ephesians 2:8-9)

Christ and His sacrifice on the cross on our behalf is the deep taproot of the doctrine of our faith.

All other philosophies wither and shrivel before the awesome radiance of God because they do not have this strong taproot at their core. Yet for those of us firmly rooted in the forgiveness and mercy of Christ, we bask in that light and flourish under its warm and loving glow.

Some things live best in the darkness. We have all heard about pale fish with blind eyes swimming in the depths of the abyss, as well as mushrooms and fungi feeding on the death and rot of the forest floor.

Tea plants, however, are not such creatures; they love the light. Shade is harmful to them and stunts their productivity. They yearn for rays of sunshine instead. (See John 3:19-20)

- Are we basking and flourishing in the sunshine of God's presence? Do we yearn for it, "as the deer pants for streams of water?" (See Psalm 42:1)

- If we find that we are wilting, could it be that we have placed our faith in something other than Christ—perhaps even unconsciously—such as our own strengths and abilities? Is it time to reach deeper, by reaching out to Him?

- On the other hand, if we find that our growth in Christ is stunted, could it be that we are living too much in the shadow of sin?

- Are we willing to come out from under that shadow, or do we find the shade comfortable?

- Perhaps it is merely a little rest or diversion from the work God has called us to do—sins of omission rather than commission? Can neglecting to do the things we *should do* damage our spiritual health and growth as much as doing things we *shouldn't?* (see Romans 7:18-19)

- It doesn't require a big towering tree to cast shade in our lives. Are there smaller things that are casting a bit of shade in a corner of your life? Are tiny little weeds, with just a few scraggly leaves, stunting you? Is it time to pull those weeds, so that you may flourish as God intends?

- Passages such as Galatians 5:19-23 and Ephesians 4:31-32 list some things God would consider weeds and others He'd consider good fruit. Can you think of additional attitudes or actions that belong on either list?

Chapter 4 – Firmly Rooted

Jesus also used the analogy of roots when He told the parable of the sower in Luke 8:5-15.

- New believers are usually excited about their faith. Because of their enthusiasm, and because of their more recent and direct contact with "the world," we often look to them to lead the charge in evangelism. Is this the best strategy, given what we know about firm roots?

- Who then should be leading out in evangelism? Is this what we actually see taking place within the Church?

- Have we become "choked with worries and riches and pleasures?" Those things can affect our fruit bearing in more than one way. How so?

- If this is the case, how can we fix it? Are we willing to set aside these things to pursue Him? Are we willing to "produce a crop a hundred times as great?"

God is the Master Gardener. He is constantly at work cultivating, nurturing, pruning, and harvesting. May we become firmly planted in Him with deep roots both within our minds and within our hearts.

- Scripture -
Colossians 2:16-23

Therefore no one is to act as your judge in regard to food or drink or in respect to a festival or a new moon or a Sabbath day—things which are a mere shadow of what is to come; but the substance belongs to Christ.

Let no one keep defrauding you of your prize by delighting in self-abasement and the worship of the angels, taking his stand on visions he has seen, inflated without cause by his fleshly mind, and not holding fast to the head, from whom the entire body, being supplied and held together by the joints and ligaments, grows with a growth which is from God.

If you have died with Christ to the elementary principles of the world, why, as if you were living in the world, do you submit yourself to decrees, such as, "Do not handle, do not taste, do not touch!" (which all refer to things destined to perish with use)—in accordance with the commandments and teachings of men?

These are matters which have, to be sure, the appearance of wisdom in self-made religion and self-abasement and severe treatment of the body, but are of no value against fleshly indulgence.

.

– Chapter 5 –
Artificial Ingredients

There are six things that go into making milk chocolate: cocoa powder, cocoa butter, vanilla, lecithin, sugar, and powdered milk.

If you want dark chocolate, which tastes more bitter, remove the milk. If you want white chocolate, remove the cocoa powder. In similar fashion, if you want chocolate peanuts, add peanuts. Chocolate toffee, add toffee.

Every recipe has its ingredients. Take away an ingredient, and you have something entirely different. Add an ingredient, and you get something else as well. To be sure, they may be similar products, but they aren't identical.

- What if you made substitutions to the chocolate recipe above—ketchup instead of powdered milk, for instance—would that work? What if you added non-food items, like sand instead of vanilla?

- Have you ever made these kinds of mistakes in the kitchen? Did you serve the altered recipe to guests before realizing your mistake? What was the result?

When it comes to the gospel message, there are two basic errors that people make. The first is to remove ingredients. The second is to add them.

That's the problem Paul addresses in this passage in Colossians: the attempt some were making to add dietary and holiday rules to the gospel.

- What are some ingredients that people have tried to remove from the gospel over the years?

- Was Christ's divinity one of your answers? Unbelievers commonly claim that Christ was a wise teacher, but not God. Does He give us this option?

- What about miracles? Thomas Jefferson cut all the miracles out of his Bible. Do modern philosophers do the same by trying to explain the miracles away?

- What about sin? People like to reclassify certain trendy or popular sins as non-sins, so that they can keep doing them without repentance or guilt. Can you think of a few modern examples? Does "tolerance" benefit the sinner in the long run?

- What about the concept of Hell and eternal separation from God? Do people sometimes try to deny these things? What would be their motivation?

Chapter 5 – Artificial Ingredients

When you walk through the streets of Rome and review its history through its art, there are a few interesting things that come to light. For example, the way angels are depicted during the rule of Constantine is very ambiguous. The angels are neither the chubby little Cupids of Greek mythology, nor the frightful giants of the Bible who must constantly say, "Do not be afraid!"

They are a blend.

Constantine wanted both his pagan population and his ever-growing Christian population to be able to look at the very same artwork and still feel comfortable. Likewise, idols built to gods and goddesses were not torn down, but merely relabeled as patron saints. The pagans would recognize the statue and ignore the label. The Christians would find comfort in the new label, but eventually began praying to dead saints instead of the risen Christ!

The Catholic Church has been around a long time and has sampled a wide variety of added ingredients: Rosary beads are a direct copy of the Hindu "Japa Mala" prayer beads. The elevation of Mary to that of near deity status was an effort to reach out to women by emulating the pagan ideal of male and female co-divinities, such as sun and moon, yin and yang. Santeria, with its merger of voodoo and Catholicism, is just another, more exotic example of this blending.

- The early church struggled with Jewish believers wanting to subject Gentile believers to Jewish law. They wanted Christianity to be a blend of Christ's redemption on the cross plus the old laws. What did the early church decide? (See Acts 15:29)

- What are some other examples of this early struggle? Do you recall Peter's vision? (See Acts 10:9-16)

- What about more recent examples of added ingredients within the Protestant Church? Baptism to be saved? Speaking in tongues to be saved? Have you heard of Theonomy or God's economy with its call for a return to Mosaic Law?

- Do our churches today sometimes add things to make the gospel more comfortable or palatable for unbelievers?

- What about within our own lives? Do we place our faith in Christ alone—or in Christ *plus*? Have we elevated certain decisions in our life to a higher status than they deserve? Dietary decisions, maybe? Politics? Homeschooling, family planning, or patriarchy? Our good works?

It seems that keeping the gospel message both pure and simple has been a struggle since the dawn of Christianity. It is a struggle that has continued through the ages and is alive and well in our own lives.

Pray that God would give you wisdom to neither add to nor take away from the glorious work done by Christ on the cross.

- Scripture -
Colossians 3:1-4

Therefore, if you have been raised up with Christ, keep seeking the things above, where Christ is seated at the right hand of God.

Set your mind on the things above, not on the things that are on earth, for you have died and your life is hidden with Christ in God.

When Christ, who is our life, is revealed, then you also will be revealed with Him in glory.

– Chapter 6 –
Total War

When a country engages in Total War, all of its resources and every ounce of its strength is focused and dedicated to the war effort. Every citizen from oldest to youngest is conscripted into service in some shape, form, or fashion.

There are no luxury items. Every meal is rationed. Curfews are strictly enforced, for even time is a precious resource.

Nothing and no one belongs to themselves in times of Total War. It is "all for one, and one for all" in a life or death struggle for existence. The enemy will give no quarter and expects none in return.

- Can you think of some examples from history when a country has engaged in total war?

- Did the majority of citizens consider their cause to be just and necessary and, therefore, worth the effort and sacrifice?

- Consider what you know about World War 2. Do you recall Rosie the Riveter?

- Why were women needed to work in the factories?

- What were they making?

- Where were the men?

- What were some of the things rationed in WW2?

- How were "Victory Gardens" and "Knitting Bees" important to the war effort?

- Have you known older family members or friends who were still hoarding odd things like rubber bands over half a century later?

- Were they combatants or did they serve the war effort in other ways?

- What are some other ways the war left an imprint on them?

Chapter 6 – Total War

Not all wars are total wars. Many modern military actions aren't even considered wars at all, but are given names like "conflicts" or "interventions."

Only a small subset of the population is required for these "engagements," usually in the form of professional soldiers and contractors.

- Can you think of some examples of smaller wars or conflicts?

- Since not everyone participates, do the majority of citizens need to agree on the justness or necessity of these types of military action?

- Think of the Vietnam War in contrast to WW2. Was everyone committed to the Vietnam War?

- Did the combatants receive support and appreciation?

- How did the lack of agreement on the "justness" and "necessity" of the war affect the national morale?

- Did this conflict also leave an "imprint?"

- Was it a good one?

As we look at the first few verses of Colossians 3, we see phrases like, *"keep seeking the things above,"* and *"set your mind on the things above."* (Some translations use the words *"heart"* or *"affections"* here, instead.)

The passage tells us that we *"have died"* and our lives are *"hidden with Christ in God."*

We are exhorted to not set our minds *"on the things that are on earth."*

- Does this sound like a limited engagement or a total commitment?

- Is it possible to become "so heavenly minded that we are no earthly good?"

- Is it possible to become "so earthly minded that we are no heavenly good?"

- Which is better? (see 1 Corinthians 9:24-25, Matthew 6:19-20)

- Do we have to choose? (see Joshua 24:14-15, Luke 16:13,)

- Do our lives show that we have chosen already?

- What are some things we might need to ration or repurpose to the Kingdom cause if we have chosen a total commitment? Money? Time? Mental energy? Talent? All of the above?

Chapter 6 – Total War

Psalms 90:12 reads, *"Teach us to number our days, that we may gain a heart of wisdom."*

Statistically speaking, if you are 35 and healthy, you have roughly 50 more Christmases to celebrate this side of heaven. You have 2,600 more Sunday mornings to worship with your fellow believers here on earth.

If your parents are in their 70's they may only have 10-15 more birthdays, anniversaries, or other holidays to celebrate with you before they begin to celebrate them with our Lord.

- Since our time on earth is limited, how does the idea of "curfews" or time management fit into the Christian worldview?

- Christ exhorts us not to worry about tomorrow (Matthew 6:34). Is it possible to "number our days" without worrying?

- Is it okay to make plans, so long as we use the caveat, *"If the Lord wills?"* (James 4:15)

- Are there some things of which we must say, "Ain't got time for that?"

- With what activities do you personally feel the need to limit your time and involvement?

- Are these "time-wasters" the same for all of us, or will they differ from person to person?

Many people think of time or resource management in terms of a pyramid. The most important things are at the top and the least important at the bottom. Most Christians, for instance, would place God at the top of such a pyramid, family and friends in the middle, and work and play towards the bottom.

An alternative view is to look at life as a pie chart. The pie is divided up into different slices. One slice might be family. Another slice would be friends. Yet another would be work, or hobbies, or volunteer work.

In this analogy, God would not be a slice at all, because God owns the entire pie. He doesn't just want the first slice or the biggest slice. He wants the whole thing.

God is not the *most important* thing. He is the *only* thing. Everything else in life is but another opportunity to serve Him.

- If you drew a pie chart of your life, what would be some of the slices?

- Would some of the slices grow or shrink at different periods in your life? School might be a huge slice early in life, but be very small later on. Can you think of other examples where the allocated portion changes?

- Does this alternate viewpoint seem to fit with Scripture? Does it make the idea of total commitment fit better?

- Look at each slice individually. Are there ways to creatively use each one for God's glory? Can

you eat and sleep in ways that glorify God? (See
1 Corinthians 10:31)

• Think about all the other responsibilities and
activities that lay claim to your time. Are there
God honoring ways to relate to your spouse?
Parent your children? Keep house? Do your job?
Surf the Internet? Coach little league? Shop for
groceries? Be a neighbor? Drive a car?

God requires a total commitment. He has purchased
us with His own blood. We are no longer our own, but
"have been bought with a price." (1 Corinthians 6:20)

Every aspect of our life, each facet, both great and
small, belongs to God. Isn't it time to lay everything on the
altar for Him, just as He laid everything on the altar for you?
Isn't it time to declare Total War? (Ephesians 6:10-13)

- Scripture -
Colossians 3:5-16

Therefore consider the members of your earthly body as dead to immorality, impurity, passion, evil desire, and greed, which amounts to idolatry.

For it is because of these things that the wrath of God will come upon the sons of disobedience, and in them you also once walked, when you were living in them.

But now you also, put them all aside: anger, wrath, malice, slander, and abusive speech from your mouth.

Do not lie to one another, since you laid aside the old self with its evil practices, and have put on the new self who is being renewed to a true knowledge according to the image of the One who created him—a renewal in which there is no distinction between Greek and Jew, circumcised and uncircumcised, barbarian, Scythian, slave and freeman, but Christ is all, and in all.

So, as those who have been chosen of God, holy and beloved, put on a heart of compassion, kindness, humility, gentleness and patience; bearing with one another, and forgiving each other, whoever has a complaint against anyone; just as the Lord forgave you, so also should you.

Life's Big Questions: Colossians

Beyond all these things put on love, which is the perfect bond of unity.

Let the peace of Christ rule in your hearts, to which indeed you were called in one body; and be thankful.

Let the word of Christ richly dwell within you, with all wisdom teaching and admonishing one another with psalms and hymns and spiritual   songs,   singing   with thankfulness in your hearts to God.

– Chapter 7 –
Running to Win

The Chicago marathon is the second largest marathon in the world, just behind the New York City marathon.

Every fall, roughly forty thousand runners gather in the streets of the Windy City near the shore of Lake Michigan. Banners with estimated finishing times are held aloft at intervals along the streets so that runners can sort themselves according to speed. The faster runners are at the front, the slower runners are at the back.

People—male and female, young and old—fill the roads as far as the eye can see. The excitement is palpable and nervous chatter fills the cool morning air. Everyone is grabbing a last minute drink or stretching one final time.

Then, there is an announcement: the race is about to begin. A hush falls on the crowd. Suddenly you hear it—the sound of a horn, high and loud. The giant snake of humanity begins to writhe and slither forward, slowly at first, then faster. The race has begun.

This scene is repeated nearly every weekend somewhere in the world. The location and the size of the event may vary, but the essence and the purpose are the same: complete a marathon.

Everyone has trained, everyone is dressed appropriately, and everyone is hoping to finish well.

Now imagine, if you will, that some prankster has tied your shoelaces together. Just as the crowd surges forward and you start to take that first step of the race, you find yourself tripping and flailing, knocking over other nearby runners as you go sprawling to the ground.

You awkwardly get up, apologizing to all around, but as soon as you try to run again, you crash to ground once more, bowling over a few more of your fellow runners.

At this point, you realize that something is amiss. You didn't "just trip" the first time. One of the aggravated runners you knocked over points out that your shoes are tied together, and you look down. Sure enough, that is the problem. Now you must decide. Do you try to run the rest of the race in slow, shuffling steps, falling over every so often despite your best efforts, or do you take some time to untangle your shoelaces?

- What is the logical response to this situation?

- Suppose you tried to complete the race with your shoes tied together. What would the other racers think of you? What percentage would even notice your struggle? What percentage of those who did notice would try to point out your problem? Would you be irritated with or grateful for the ones who pointed it out?

- Would any of the other racers try to stop and help you untangle the shoelaces? Would they be able to do so, if you just kept shuffling along?

In this passage in Colossians, we are encouraged to put aside a whole variety of sins in which we "once walked."

We find a similar admonition in the book of Hebrews:

> *"Therefore, since we have so great a cloud of witnesses surrounding us, let us also lay aside every encumbrance and the sin which so easily entangles us, and let us run with endurance the race that is set before us."* (Hebrews 12:1)

- Can you list the entangling sins Paul mentions in the Colossians passage?

- Are any of these sins things that you struggle with? How does that struggle affect your Christian walk and witness?

- Are there sins not listed here that you struggle with? What will it take for you to lay them aside?

- Are any of these sins things someone you know struggles with? How might you help disentangle them?

- Do your own struggles with sin keep you from effectively helping others gain victory over theirs? What is your responsibility toward them? Toward yourself? (Compare Luke 6:41-42, Galatians 6:1-2, 1 John 1:7-9)

When sin trips us up, we are often hurt in the process. However, we can inadvertently hurt others, as well, because none of us is ever truly running alone.

- Who is more likely to cause a bigger "pile up" when they fall, a runner at the front or a runner at the back?

- Can you think of runners at the forefront of Christianity who have fallen and caused a domino effect?

- Did natural ability or proper training do them much good when their shoelaces were tied together?

- If you were to fall, who in your life would you likely "knock over?"

- Are those people worth protecting, even if you aren't "worried about yourself?"

- Is it enough to apologize and seek forgiveness when we trip up, or are we called to untangle our shoelaces, as well, by repenting and "putting aside" our sin?

- How seriously will God and our fellow man take our apologies, if we refuse to address underlying problems?

Chapter 7 – Running to Win

The second part of the passage lists the things we should do, as opposed to the things we shouldn't do.

- Can you name the positive things Christians are here encouraged to do?

- Are any of these things difficult for you? If so, why do you think that is?

- If we consider repentance of sin to be an untangling of our shoelaces so that we can walk and eventually run, might we consider these positive things as proper training, proper form, and proper attire for the race?

- The last thing on the list is "admonishing one another." Does this involve helping other runners who have tripped up?

- Should we simply point out their problem or try to give them a hand?

- Will they be grateful? Does their gratitude or lack thereof change our responsibility?

Christ calls us to repentance. He commands us to turn away from the old sins that so easily entangle us. He also calls us to put on a new life, one that is exemplified by love and compassion for those around us. Such a life is not a sprint, but a marathon. Yet the God who calls us to this kind of life also equips and empowers us to win.

- Scripture -
Colossians 3:18-21

Wives, be subject to your husbands, as is fitting in the Lord.

Husbands, love your wives and do not be embittered against them.

Children, be obedient to your parents in all things, for this is well-pleasing to the Lord.

Fathers, do not exasperate your children, so that they will not lose heart.

– Chapter 8 –
The Dog that Didn't Bark

There is a famous scene in one of the many Sherlock Holmes stories, where Holmes is speaking to a Scotland Yard detective, named Gregory:

> Gregory: *"Is there any other point to which you would wish to draw my attention?"*
> Holmes: *"To the curious incident of the dog in the night-time."*
> Gregory: *"The dog did nothing in the night-time."*
> Holmes: *"That was the curious incident."*

Because the guard dog did <u>not</u> bark, Holmes deduces that the dog must have known the intruder, and is thus able to solve the case. It was the absence of something, rather than its presence, that provided the biggest clue in solving the mystery.

As we look at Paul's instructions regarding family relationships in Colossians, there is one relationship he conspicuously does not address at all.

- Which immediate family relationship goes unaddressed?

- Why do you think Paul doesn't feel the need to discuss a mother's love toward her children?

- Is mother's love a unique bond? Have you ever seen the news when they interview the mother of some horrible criminal and she tries to convince the reporter that "her baby" would never do whatever it is that her baby is convicted of doing?

- Is a mother's natural affection for her children or her protective instincts toward them enough to ensure she always acts in their best interest?

- Paul does briefly mention the mother/child relationship in a later letter to Titus, where he writes,

  > *"Older women... [are to teach] the young women to love their husbands, to love their children, to be sensible, pure, workers at home, kind, being subject to their own husbands, so that the word of God will not be dishonored...." (Titus 2:3-5)*

  Why do you suppose he gives older women the responsibility of teaching these things? Does he expect them to teach younger women by word or by example—or both?

Chapter 8 – The Dog that Didn't Bark

Scripture rarely tells us to do things that God has wired us to do instinctively. Rather, Scripture commands us to do those things that don't come naturally and therefore require supernatural strength to carry out. It is by requiring the difficult, and often the seemingly impossible, that God teaches us to depend on Him.

When Christ commands us in Matthew 22:39 to "Love your neighbor as yourself," there is an underlying assumption that loving ourselves is something we naturally do already. The unnatural or difficult part is to love our neighbor in a similar fashion.

That directive is so at odds with our innate selfishness that we actually cannot do it in our own strength. We must depend on Christ to supernaturally love others through us in a way that is utterly impossible for us to do alone.

The most interesting thing about allowing Christ to love others *through us* is that we ourselves are blessed in the process. And that makes sense. If you are going around spreading supernatural sunshine and love, some of that goodness is going to reflect back on you from the people you love.

But even more important is the bond of dependence and the deepening relationship you develop with the Lord in the process. You are becoming more fully alive as you are filled with the Source of all life. You are becoming more fully yourself as you are empowered by the One who made you uniquely you.

As we look at the handful of instructions given to us by Paul regarding family relationships, let us look at what *isn't* said as well as what *is* said.

Further, let us keep in mind that we are the ultimate beneficiaries of each of these commands as Christ empowers us to carry them out.

- What does Paul instruct wives to do?

- Being "subject" is a very unpopular concept with many women today. Is this unpopularity unique to our "modern" times?

- Does anyone—male or female, young or old—naturally want to submit to anyone or anything else? Is this just a "women's issue," or is it actually a "people issue?"

- If God is asking women (or anyone else, for that matter) to do something that does not come easily for them, He must have a reason. What practical reasons jump to mind as a possibility for this instruction? What are some spiritual benefits of this instruction?

- Is "being subject" just a tool for solving disagreements or is it bigger than that? What are some ways a wife can be subject to her husband in a broader, more complete way?

- Why aren't women instructed to *love* their husbands in this passage?

Chapter 8 – The Dog that Didn't Bark

Men are given three instructions, not just one. Two concern their wives and one concerns their children.

- What are Paul's two instructions to husbands concerning wives?

- If men need to be told to love their wives, the implication is that loving them must be difficult or uncomfortable on some level. In what ways is it difficult for men to love their wives? Who alone can help husbands to overcome these difficulties?

- Likewise, men are told not to be embittered against their wives. Again, the implication is that they will naturally tend towards bitterness. Why might a husband become embittered?

- The Bible repeatedly warns of the dangers of bitterness. A great quote by Joanna Weaver sums it up nicely: "Bitterness is like drinking poison and waiting for the other person to die." Who, then, is the ultimate winner when we get rid of bitterness?

- What is the instruction to fathers concerning children?

- How might fathers exasperate their children? How do we overcome these tendencies? Does planning and intentionality have a role? Does the Holy Spirit play a part?

Finally, children are given one command.

- What is that one command?

- Is it instinctive for children to do this?

- When they are small, do children have the benefit of rationality to help them understand this commandment? Do they have the benefit of the Holy Spirit prior to becoming Christians?

- Who then must help them obey the command to obey? How are parents to do this?

- Does this give insight into how God must deal with us prior to our salvation and maturation in the Lord?

- Can this give our children insight into the nature of God, as we represent Him to our children?

All of God's commands have a practical benefit as well as a spiritual benefit. The practical benefit is often the most obvious, but the spiritual benefit is invariably the most important.

The thing we must keep in mind is that God loves us and wants our good. Although obedience to His commands seldom comes naturally, it is this very "unnaturalness" that forces us to supernaturally depend on Him.

– *Scripture* –
Colossians 3:17, 22-25; 4:1

Whatever you do in word or deed, do all in the name of the Lord Jesus, giving thanks through Him to God the Father....

Slaves, in all things obey those who are your masters on earth, not with external service, as those who merely please men, but with sincerity of heart, fearing the Lord.

Whatever you do, do your work heartily, as for the Lord rather than for men, knowing that from the Lord you will receive the reward of the inheritance. It is the Lord Christ whom you serve.

For he who does wrong will receive the consequences of the wrong which he has done, and that without partiality.

Masters, grant to your slaves justice and fairness, knowing that you too have a Master in heaven.

– Chapter 9 –
Exceeding Expectations

Near the turn of the last century, America was at war with Spain, and President McKinley needed to get a message to a man named Garcia, who was the leader of a group of Cuban rebels.

Unfortunately, no one seemed to know exactly where in the thick island jungle the rebels were hiding. It fell to a man named Rowan to carry a letter to Garcia from the President of the United States.

Rowan took the letter, traveled to Cuba, and disappeared into the dense tropical foliage. He traveled on foot and in the darkness of night.

Several weeks later, he reemerged. His message having been delivered, he carried a response in his hand. Against all odds and without question or complaint, he had done what he was asked to do.

A journalist by the name of Elbert Hubbard was so inspired by this difficult task being so competently carried out that he wrote a short essay about it in 1899. The essay compared the quiet efficiency of the message bearer, Rowan, to that of the average American worker at the time.

The contrast was stark and anything but favorable to the typical employee of the time, yet the story seemed to resonate with the people who read it.

The essay was soon reproduced and began to spread. It grew into a pamphlet and then a book. Over 40 million people across the world read its message.

And its message was this: Good workers are hard to find. We need more men and women in this world who can be counted on to "carry a message to Garcia."

Eventually, there were several movie renditions and "carrying a message to Garcia" became synonymous with doing your job and doing it well.

Over a hundred years have passed since the story was first told, but the need for competent, dependable, hard working people has not changed.

- Have you ever had to hire someone to work for you, even just for housekeeping, yard work, or babysitting?

- What are some of the things you worry about as an employer when you hire someone new?

- Do you ever find yourself expecting the worst, while hoping for the best?

- Have you ever had to fire someone? What was the reason? Was it difficult, even if justified?

- Is there someone at your company or job who is the "go to" person?

- What is so special about that person?

- Would you say that person exceeds expectations for the position that he/she is in?

- Would your company be better off if there were more employees like that?

- Are those kind of people born or made?

- Are the Christians where you work known as the best, most dependable and diligent workers? Should they be?

- What is *your* reputation at work? Do you exceed expectations? Do you set the standard of excellence?

- How does the quality of your work affect your Christian witness?

- Dorothy Sayers went so far as to claim that a believer cannot do shoddy work without "bringing Christianity into contempt." Do you agree?

As we look at this passage in Colossians, Paul is addressing the extreme case of masters and slaves, so common at that time. The modern equivalent might be management and labor.

In the early days of America, the difference between managers and masters was very small. Young children would work long hours in squalid conditions for such low pay that their lives were virtually indistinguishable from those of slaves. It is still that way in some corners of the earth today, but is fortunately becoming less and less so. Christians have often led the charge in giving a voice to the voiceless and improving conditions for the oppressed.

- What is the worst job you ever had or heard of?

- How do these worst case scenarios compare to what you know of slavery? How are they the same? How are they different?

- Should Christians advocate for those being mistreated? What if *you* are being mistreated? Is there a God-honoring way for you to advocate for yourself?

- What is the best job you ever had or heard about? If you include hobbies or volunteer work, does that change your answer?

- How big a role did your "boss" or immediate supervisor play in making the job good or bad? Did your co-workers have an effect? How about the work itself?

Chapter 9 – Exceeding Expectations

Paul tells workers to work "as for the Lord," since it is actually Christ whom they serve.

- How does working for Christ instead of "the man" change our approach to our work? Our attitude about work?

- Who wins when we take this better approach? Our boss? Ourselves? Christ?

- Does our work ethic—the way we do the jobs assigned to us—reflect on our faith?

- Have you ever been laid off or been out of work? Were you glad to be employed again?

- Did you have a new attitude about work afterwards?

- Is there a different mindset between "*having* to do" something and "*getting* to do" something?

- Is your mindset one of having to work or is it one of getting to serve Christ through your work?

Paul tells masters to treat their slaves with fairness and justice. After all, the masters also have a "Master in heaven" who measures out to them in the same manner that they measure things out to others. (See Matthew 7:2)

Modern business practice talks about internal and external fairness in pay. Internal fairness means that pay is similar for similar jobs within a company and external fairness means that pay is similar for similar jobs at competing companies.

When a company is internally and externally fair, workers are actually happier and do better work. Companies that pay slightly more than their competition get even more loyalty and even better work from their employees.

The opposite is true for companies that are "under the market" in pay.

- Pay is just one aspect of fairness and justice to employees. What are some other ways an employer can bless their employees?

- There are both practical and spiritual benefits to God's commands. Can you name some practical benefits of fairness and justice, whether in pay or otherwise?

- What might be the spiritual benefits to an employer who is fair and just?

- Do employees expect fairness and justice, or do they also expect the worst, while hoping for the best?

Chapter 9 – Exceeding Expectations

- Does being a good boss honor God in a similar manner as being a good employee?

- Can a boss exceed expectations, as well?

- Are the Christian leaders at your job known for fairness and justice? Should they be? Are you?

Many employers assume their employees will be lazy and dishonest. When Christians are honest and hardworking, they exceed their employer's expectations and thus honor Christ. In similar manner, employers who are fair and just are also exceeding expectations and honoring Christ.

Both Christian employers and Christian employees are "carrying a message" to the world. May all of us who carry the message of Jesus be known for doing our jobs and doing them well!

– Scripture –
Colossians 4:2-6

Devote yourselves to prayer, keeping alert in it with an attitude of thanksgiving; praying at the same time for us as well, that God will open up to us a door for the word, so that we may speak forth the mystery of Christ, for which I have also been imprisoned; that I may make it clear in the way I ought to speak.

Conduct yourselves with wisdom toward outsiders, making the most of the opportunity.

Let your speech always be with grace, as though seasoned with salt, so that you will know how you should respond to each person.

– Chapter 10 –
Power and Wisdom

We have all heard that the divorce rate amongst Christians and non-Christians alike is around fifty percent. There is some evidence that this number may be falling—not because more people are staying married, but because fewer people are bothering to get married in the first place. If you include couples who live together for a few years and then separate, the numbers go right back to that unfortunate baseline.

The one thing that has been shown to protect marriages better than anything else is prayer. Couples who pray together regularly have a divorce rate of less than one percent. Sadly, only about four percent of Christian couples actually do this (pray together regularly). If you happen to be a pastor, then that number goes up to six percent!

It seems that if we want to protect marriages, we need to teach couples to pray together. We read books, attend seminars, go to counseling, and do a myriad of other things of unknown benefit to those trying to stay married. Yet, we don't do the one thing that is virtually guaranteed to work.

- If you contracted Ebola and had a fifty-fifty chance of dying, but your doctor offered you a vaccine that would give you a greater than ninety-nine percent chance of surviving, would you take the vaccine?

- Your marriage has a fifty-fifty chance of survival, but a vaccine exists called *prayer*. Only a small percentage of married couples have actually taken this vaccine. Are you one of them? Should you be? Is today the day to start?

Of course, marriage is just one facet of the Christian experience. Perhaps the reason we lack spiritual power in other areas of our lives is because we aren't plugging into the spiritual power Source through prayer. Churches aren't lacking in plans or programs—just in prayer.

In this passage, Paul urges Christians to "devote yourselves to prayer." In fact, he encourages prayer over and over throughout all of his letters to the churches. If someone is sick, pray. If someone is in jail, pray. If someone is suffering persecution, pray. The answer to virtually every problem is the same: prayer. Even in the Old Testament, people would "call upon the name of the Lord" or "cry out to God" in times of trouble.

Prayer is a central theme of Scripture, yet it seems to be less central with modern believers and modern churches. Perhaps that is why today's Church appears so anemic. We're trying to do things in our own limited power, when what we need—now as desperately as ever—is God's supernatural power. Could it be that modern affluence and technology has tricked us into believing we can do things on our own that we actually cannot? Maybe we have all been busy building a gigantic spiritual supercomputer, but no one has bothered to plug it in.

- Is prayer a central component of your personal life?

- Is prayer a central component of your family life (spouse and children)?

- Is prayer a central component of your church's life?

- If you are not relying on God's power through prayer, what are you relying on? At work? At home? At church? Can you change?

- Consider your ability to lead the lost to Christ. Has God used you to lead anyone to Christ recently? Ever?

- Is it a lack of knowledge that is limiting your witness or a lack of power?

- Is it a lack of opportunity or a lack of perception that is holding you back?

- Are you willing to pray that God opens your eyes to the needs around you and that He gives you the power to meet those needs?

Power and perception are only a part of the equation. Wisdom, in both conduct and speech, is the other part of the equation. Paul addresses them both in the second portion of this passage.

- If a nation has empowered someone to be an ambassador to a foreign country, how is that person expected to behave while serving abroad?

- When that person speaks on behalf of his home country, should he be rude or diplomatic?

- Whom are we representing in our conduct and speech? Are we representing Him well, as good ambassadors?

- Paul uses the phrase "seasoned with salt" concerning our speech. Is salt sugary sweet? Is it bitter and offensive?

- In addition to adding flavor, salt also acts as a preservative. Could Paul be communicating the idea that we are trying to preserve relationships in the way we speak?

- Is this always possible? (See John 15:18 or Matthew 10:22)

- Should we try anyway? (See Romans 12:18)

We are ambassadors for Jesus whereever we are. We don't get to take off the uniform and just "be ourselves." We have been purchased with Christ's blood and we are no longer our own.

Our goal is to represent Him well in all that we do or say. This is a daunting task, one for which we have not the strength. God, however, does have such strength and is willing to give it to us, if only we will ask. Isn't it time to stop trying to do so much in your own power?

When it comes to your marriage, your chances of success on your own are the same as the flip of a coin. When it comes to leading others to faith, your chance of success apart from God's empowering grace drops to zero.

Isn't it time to stop treating life like a Vegas casino with the odds so heavily stacked against you and to call out to the only One Who is a sure thing?

– Scripture –
Colossians 4:7-18

As to all my affairs, Tychicus, our beloved brother and faithful servant and fellow bond-servant in the Lord, will bring you information.

For I have sent him to you for this very purpose, that you may know about our circumstances and that he may encourage your hearts; and with him Onesimus, our faithful and beloved brother, who is one of your number. They will inform you about the whole situation here.

Aristarchus, my fellow prisoner, sends you his greetings; and also Barnabas's cousin Mark (about whom you received instructions; if he comes to you, welcome him); and also Jesus who is called Justus; these are the only fellow workers for the kingdom of God who are from the circumcision, and they have proved to be an encouragement to me.

Epaphras, who is one of your number, a bondslave of Jesus Christ, sends you his greetings, always laboring earnestly for you in his prayers, that you may stand perfect and fully assured in all the will of God. For I testify for him that he has a deep concern for you and for those who are in Laodicea and Hierapolis.

Luke, the beloved physician, sends you his greetings, and also Demas.

Greet the brethren who are in Laodicea and also Nympha and the church that is in her house.

When this letter is read among you, have it also read in the church of the Laodiceans; and you, for your part read my letter that is coming from Laodicea. Say to Archippus, "Take heed to the ministry which you have received in the Lord, that you may fulfill it."

I, Paul, write this greeting with my own hand. Remember my imprisonment. Grace be with you.

- Chapter 11 -
Slave vs. Free

Have you ever looked at the list of names at the closing of Paul's letters and wondered who the people were, what was their story, and what ever happened to them?

What about all those people in the seemingly endless genealogies of the Old Testament? Ever wonder about those people? Their brief mention usually represents decades and sometimes even centuries of faithful service to God. Perhaps in heaven we will meet them and get to hear how God was with them through the good times and the bad. We will find out that even though their culture, language, and technology were very different from our own, our stories are very much alike.

One of my study Bibles has a table showing all the ancient kings of Israel. It is neatly divided into two columns: good kings and bad kings. The lists are about even.

Sometimes a king would start out good, but eventually turn away from the Lord. There was no third column offering partial credit. Like a runner who is leading the race, but trips near the finish line, these kings started out strong, but finished poorly.

In this passage, there are two characters about which we know a little bit more than usual, because they are mentioned elsewhere by Paul. One is a slave who has become free and the other is a freeman who ultimately becomes enslaved.

Let's start by looking at the slave who gains his freedom. His name is Onesimus, and he is discussed in detail in the book of Philemon. In verses 10-18 of that single chapter book, we hear Paul's plea on behalf of Onesimus, a presumably runaway slave, to Onesimus' owner, Philemon.

- When a slave runs away, does he do it in stages or all at once?

- When we turn away from the slavery of sin, is it abrupt or gradual? Does a murderer simply murder fewer people, perhaps? Or thieves rob fewer houses?

- Do we sometimes try to take this gradual approach with sins we perceive to be "lesser?" Does God want partial repentance?

- If a slave runs away, is he completely free or is there still a debt to be paid before he is truly free?

- By definition, a runaway slave is unable to purchase his own freedom. Who offers to pay for Onesimus' freedom and advocates on his behalf?

- Who advocates on behalf of sinners and offers to purchase their freedom from sin?

Chapter 11 – Slave vs. Free

Now let's turn to the freeman who becomes enslaved. His name is Demas, and Paul mentions him three times in the New Testament. In the verse 24 of Philemon, he is named alongside Mark and Luke as a "fellow worker" with Paul. What a privilege to be part of that team!

Demas is mentioned again in the passage we are currently considering, Colossians 4:14. After Paul has gone into detail about a number of the other brethren, he tacks this name to the very end, almost as an afterthought: "and also Demas."

The lack of specifics regarding Demas' service and character speaks volumes when contrasted to the attention given to his other companions in the same passage—another case of "the dog that didn't bark."

The third and final time Demas is mentioned is in 2 Timothy 4:10, where Paul writes, "for Demas, having loved this present world, has deserted me and gone to Thessalonica." Just like the Old Testament kings, Demas started strong, but finished poorly.

We have discussed that the turn from sin is abrupt. But note also that the turn towards sin usually is not. Typically, it begins with a small compromise here or there and then gradually grows and takes root. This seems to be the case with Demas and also with King Solomon.

Solomon began his career by asking God for wisdom rather than wealth or power. His great wisdom did in fact lead to wealth and power, as well. Unfortunately, as that wealth and power accrued, Solomon started to do some very unwise things. First, he began to marry foreign wives. Then he allowed those wives to worship their own false gods and to build altars to those gods. Ultimately, Solomon joined his wives in worshipping those false gods, the most foolish thing possible for such a previously wise and God-fearing man.

- Have you ever been on a diet? Did you quit the diet all at once or did you cheat a little here and there until you were cheating more than you were dieting?

- Perhaps you have heard the story of the frog in the kettle where the heat is gradually increased and the frog is slowly cooked alive without ever noticing. Can you identify areas in your life where Satan might be slowly turning up the heat without your noticing?

- Are you willing to ask God to open your eyes to these blind spots? Are you willing to get out of the "kettle" when He does?

Jesus tells the story of two sons in Matthew 21:28-31 as follows in the NIV:

> *"What do you think? There was a man who had two sons. He went to the first and said, 'Son, go and work today in the vineyard.'*
> *'I will not,' he answered, but later he changed his mind and went. Then the father went to the other son and said the same thing. He answered, 'I will, sir,' but he did not go. Which of the two did what his father wanted?"*
> *"The first," they answered. Jesus said to them, "Truly I tell you, the tax collectors and the*

prostitutes are entering the kingdom of God ahead of you."

As we conclude this series of lessons in Colossians, the big questions we must ask ourselves are these:

- Are we more like Onesimus or Demas? A slave who has an advocate and is gaining his freedom or a freeman who is becoming enslaved to sin?

- Are we more like the wise kings of the Old Testament who finish strong or more like the foolish ones who stumble at the end?

- Are we like the first son in Jesus's parable or the second?

My prayer is that each of you has found an Advocate in Christ and that He has paid your debt and freed you from sin. I pray that you run your race to completion, that you finish strong, and that you can claim the imperishable crown that awaits you at the end!

- Acknowledgements -

You can't write a Bible study guide without first and foremost thanking God for His wonderful love and mercy as manifested in His Son, Jesus Christ! He is our life, our strength, and our eternal hope.

Likewise, I want to thank my wife, Jennifer, who is not only my biggest cheerleader and fan, but also my faithful editor and graphic designer. Nothing I have written in book or blog form would exist without her unwavering assistance.

Furthermore, I want to thank Doug Morris, my pastor, for asking me to write the small group study guide for the book of Colossians for our church. I would not have written it without his encouragement. The assignment was a lot of fun, and I learned far more than I taught in the process.

Finally, thank you to my church family for actually reading the study guides week after week and providing feedback. May God richly bless all that you do!

- Doug Flanders
March 6, 2015

- About the Author -

Doug Flanders was born and raised in San Antonio, TX. He attended Dallas Baptist University, where he met his wife, Jennifer. They were married in 1987 and had their first child in 1988, shortly before Doug started medical school at UT Southwestern Health Science Center in Dallas.

By the time Doug completed his MD, he had two more children and was voted by his classmates "most likely to have a dozen kids." Not wanting to disappoint, he and Jennifer went on to have nine more!

Doug now practices anesthesia in Tyler, Texas, where he also serves as Chief of Staff at one of the largest medical centers in the region. When he isn't working or spending time with his family (which, by year's end, will have grown to include six grandchildren and two daughters-in-law), Doug reads widely and works on various writing projects. If you'd like to read more from this author, we invite you to visit his blog, www.AllTruthIsGodsTruth.com.

More Books from
– Prescott Publishing –

25 Ways to Communicate Respect to Your Husband:
A Handbook for Wives
by Jennifer Flanders

100 Days of Blessing: Volumes 1 and 2
by Nancy Campbell

From Feminism to Fertility
by Michelle Kauenhofen

Get Up & Go:
Fun Ideas for Getting Fit as a Family
by Jennifer Flanders

Glad Tidings: The First 25 Years
of Flanders Family Christmas Letters
by Jennifer Flanders

How to Encourage Your Husband
by Nancy Campbell

Love Your Husband/ Love Yourself:
Embracing God's Purpose for Passion in Marriage
by Jennifer Flanders

Moment by Moment: A Devotional Journal for Girls
by Jennifer Flanders

More Books by
– Doug Flanders –

25 Ways to Show Love to Your Wife

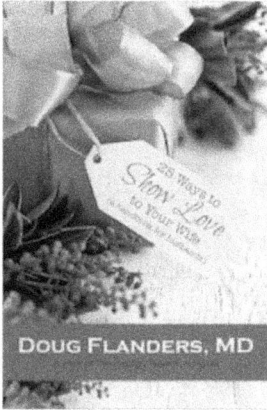

Your wife is a reflection of your love for her. If you would like her to be more joyful and affectionate, more respectful, and more appreciative of all you do, then you must learn to treat her as you'd like to be treated. This book outlines twenty-five tried and true ways to do exactly that, with practical suggestions at the end of each chapter for putting the principles into practice.

The Prodigy Project: A Novel

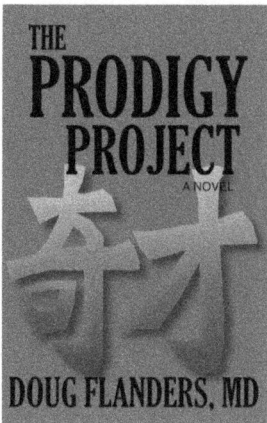

When a terrifying new bio-weapon threatens to destroy civilization as we know it, an unconventional hero is called in to stop it. Jon Gunderson, an expert in biological warfare, is also a devoted family man whose wife and kids have unwittingly accompanied him on yet another assignment. This tale torn from tomorrow's headlines will keep readers of all ages on the edge of their seats.